A Journey
from
Love to Love

A Journey
from
Love to Love

For Eva
with love and blessings —
Azima

AZIMA LILA FOREST

A Journey from love to Love
Copyright ©2017 Azima Lila Forest

ISBN: 978-1-940769-76-9
Publisher: Mercury HeartLink
Printed in the United States of America

Contact the author at: *azima@zianet.com*

Mercury HeartLink
www.heartlink.com

1   Acknowledgements

3   Dedication

7   Preface

8   The Dream

10   Catching Fire

12   Love's Fool

14   A Day At Muir Beach

16   My Other Life

18   Dedication

20   Love Offering

22   Moment of Truth

24   Heart Weather

26   Solve et Coagula

28   Early Winter Lament

30   Pilgrimage

32   Something Beautiful for Allah

34   Al Haqq

36   Al Baqi

38   1° Aquarius, Scorpio Moon

40   Message to Myself

42   Parable in Flight

44   Masaje de Curación

46   Migrations

48   Buried Treasure

50   Ya Muakhkhir

52   Ad-Darr

54   Ieri Oggi Domani

56   On Retreat

66   Fana-fi-Ishk

68   On Hearing "Sleeping Beauty"

70   A Wider View

72   Fana-fi-Lillah

74   The Waters

76   A New Rhythm

78   Layers

80   It Becomes True

82   A Gathering of Sufis

84   Hu Knows

86   The Border Country

88   Prayer

90   Water Blessing

92   A Wider World of Love

94   A Wish Come True

96   Al Qahhar

98   The Darshan Tree

100   Magnificat

102   Ishk

107   Glossary

113   About the Author

Acknowledgements

With deepest gratitude to all my Sufi teachers, especially Hazrat Pir Moineddin Jablonski (pbuh), Murshid Wali Ali Meyer, Murshid Mariam Baker, and Murshid Saadi Shakur Chishti.

To my Silver City poetry circle, who mentored me in the process of bringing a wild collection of heart cries into something hopefully worthy of sharing with you.

With great thanks to Stewart Warren for helping me bring the images in my mind and heart into this form.

With heartfelt love to the soul sisters whose friendship saw me through this amazing time.

To the Beloved One
who was the one all along

عشق الله معبود الله

Ishk Allah Mahboud Lillah

God Is Love, Lover, and Beloved

Preface

Years ago, I awoke from a dream in the middle of the night to find myself deeply in love with someone I had known for many years. He didn't return the feelings I had for him, and so began a long and intense journey of ecstasy and pain, as I was thrown headlong into the ocean of love.

The poems in this book were written over that period of three years. I share them here in the hopes that this chronicle in poetry will touch individual hearts undergoing an experience such as this, and be a source of recognition and hope. As I see it, we are all born to know and experience the Love of Allah, the Source, Being, and Destiny of all, and we come to know this Love through the experience of loving other human beings.

For those readers not familiar with the Sufi terminology found in some of the poems, there is a glossary at the back.

May this offering be of benefit to all beings.

The Dream

A gathering of friends
joined in a circle
a great light
a touch
an image from a long-ago life
a spirit voice
naming me teacher

Catching Fire

A dream – a flash of lightning
the kindling in my heart catches fire
shock and surprise!
the Arousing, Thunder
the fire is bright, often smoky
with much pain of longing

I pray with whole-heart
the fire turns to light
for awhile, peace and bliss
surrender
acceptance
exaltation
wanting only
the happiness of the beloved

For awhile

Now the longing begins again
pray again

Round
And round
each time around

the heart is softened
a little more

Unwilling to leave the dance floor
the threshing floor
i wonder
can i pray for a turning
to something higher?
Not yet
Not yet

But something within
longs to be burned up completely
and the ashes blown away
by the Breath of the Beloved

Love's Fool

Who is this crazy fool
crying her heart's tears
at music and poetry
the world's pain
and her own longing?

She seemed so balanced
so calm and mature
until that journey
to the place of kindling
until that earth-quaking dream!

Now look at her!
whispering in the night
writing poems
wandering the house in the wee hours
singing
giving thanks for her undoing

A Day At Muir Beach

Clear September sky
warm sand and sunlight
the healing roar
of Mother Ocean
endlessly rocking

An ordinary afternoon in paradise
Sunday people
out with their dogs
their kids
friends
mates
lovers

Me? don't want no dog
don't have no kids
not any more
friends? Oh yes
priceless treasures in my life
mate? lover?
nope
Just one beloved
far far away

My life is different
from these
and yet
just the same
we all live and love
and want to be loved

If only we knew
kow deeply are ARE loved
this earth would reveal itself
as the Paradise
it Really Is

Mother Ocean
rock me gently
into the realization
of True Love
that i may live it
and share it
with all

My Other Life

The rhythm of my days
Goes on as always

Morning practices and prayers
breakfast on the porch
preparing for the work of the day

Post office, spreadsheet, database
calendars and schedules
meetings and errands
and ordinary household things

The rhythm of my days
goes on as always

But in and around and through it all
in the space between heartbeats
the pulse of this love
beats silently
a secret second life
the real life
of my body, heart, and soul

Dedication

I have a new post
founded on a dream

Keeper of the flame
tending the sacred fire
so that it burns bright and steady
clear and quiet

Preparer of the way
holding a great spaciousness
in which this love
might grow into mutuality
if you will
If You Will

An accommodation
for love, harmony, and beauty
truth
respect, compassion, gratitude
fire and light
lightness and laughter
co-creation

and mutual unfolding
For the benefit of all

Insh'Allah
Insh'Allah
Insh'Allah

Love Offering

In the secret garden of the heart
a scarlet rosebud swells
slowly opens its outer petals to the sun
revealing layer after layer

Toward the center
a tinge of pink
paler
more delicate

Now fully open
at its heart
a pure white offering
to the beloved
and the Beloved

Passion
tenderness
willing surrender
all displayed
in one perfect bloom

Moment of Truth

After months of longing
struggling
to keep that longing contained
on this side
of the rainbow bridge
between our hearts
i see
that this desire for union
has suffused
my every communication

Now I stand bereft
of any personal response
cold consequence
of my passionate impatience
to share my inner world
with him

Ah
i see
my impulsiveness
has ridden rough-shod
over my wise self's knowing
that this is not the time

The young self within
who longs to be loved
and can't believe
it's possible
hitched a ride
on the back of
unconditional love
who wants only
the well-being of the beloved

Lesson learned
bitter medicine taken
what to do?
love that young one
into Love
put my forehead to the floor
Be the silent moon
bearing witness to his sun

Heart Weather

Yesterday
the sun shone all day long

In here
a rain of tears fell all through the day and night

Today
the sky is gray

In here
the heart-sun is shining brightly
all the pain of not-having and no-hope
washed away

Today love reigns
and nothing can dim its radiance

Blessed be
the rain and the sun

Solve et Coagula

Love forces me
to look at the naked face
of the wounding presence
of patterns shaped in childhood
separation, rejection, alienation

Love forces me
to drink this bitter medicine
the healing presence
of the alchemy of the heart
dissolution, re-formation, unity

Love shows me
a brilliant flash of light
the energy that will be released
in this process of transmutation

Love, give me the courage
to see it through

Early Winter Lament

Naked boughs, faded grass, cold, cold air
this body suffers
chilled to the bone

Where is warmth? Love?

I continue
to hold the vision
with hope
without hope

Am I patient, persistent, flexible and strong,
or only stubborn and deluded?

Lao Tzu asks
"Can you have the patience to wait
'till the mud settles and the water is clear?"

Moineddin says "Trust!"

I take my medicine often
Ya Sabur, Ya Matin, Ya Azim

Insh'Allah
this will get me though the long cold winter

Pilgrimage

The brilliance of awakening
Is over

I have entered onto the pilgrimage of Love
in earnest
the way is arduous now

The path is steep and lonely
rough and treacherous
everything is dim and wet
low-lying clouds of unknowing
surround me

The only light or warmth anywhere
comes from my heart
from the beacon illuminating
just the next step

My sole companion is the voice
of the One inside
saying
one more step
one more step

Once in awhile
a ministering angel stops by
responding to a cry for help
and whispers words of encouragement

Although I cannot see it
i know there is a great Light
at the top of the mountain

This is all I know

Something Beautiful for Allah

I 've been praying
that this lonely love
become the love of two
rare
precious
something beautiful for Allah

Suddenly I know
this love
just as it is
this moment
is
something Beautiful for Allah!

It's my secret
but the Beloved knows
sees through my eyes
hears through my ears
feels through my heart

So that's why
I was thrown in this ocean!

Al Haqq

Three things cannot long be hidden:
the sun, the moon, and the truth.
—Buddha

Rivers of tears
course down my cheeks
flow down my neck
wash over my heart

Your love is for another

I have felt this revelation
moving near
in these last days
and now it is here

I told you my truth
you responded with yours
there is love in this

I tell myself
i haven't lost you as my friend
it's only the dreams of love
that now must end

The love of lovers
is not ours to share
perhaps the love of friends
will deepen
because those dreams were there

Al Baqi

Divested of my dreams
left with unembroidered love
what is left of me?
what has God wrought?

A thinner skin
a wider view

A broken-open heart
that blesses the beloved
even so

1° Aquarius, Scorpio Moon

It's my birthday
and I'll cry if I want to

Last night a dream
of sweet shared comfort
in the company of friends

Ecstatic union at the center of the dome
a radiant ritual blessing
and finally
oh, so finally
the death
of my beloved brother-king
at the very place
where we became one

This visitation of love and death
arouses my waking-dream pain

I wear black today
on my birthday
covered by a lustrous layer
of my watery soul-color
aquamarine
inside, mourning
outside, shining

My heart balks
at the thought of celebrating
this milestone
in the company of friends
who know nothing
of this love and loss

Perhaps
their sweet presence
will help dispel
this private cloud of grief

Message to Myself

My turn again
to give the sermon
at the Fellowship

A woman struggling
with loved ones dying
had requested a reflection
on grief and loss

Yes
i said
i'll be glad to talk on that
what would the title be?
"The Ties That Bind:
Grief, Loss, and Letting Go"

Lord knows
i told myself
it's a topic I know
so very well

All this
before I knew
the death of hope
for the fulfillment
of this love

I have put off the writing
until the eleventh hour

What will the music be?
"All Things Must Pass"
George Harrison
"Love Is the Ocean"
we'll sing it together

Finally
i begin to write
i open the tap
to my heart's waters
and as always
the lessons from my own story
flow out on the screen

It is finished

I read it through
from beginning to end
this distillation
of my life and love
the perfect message to myself

Parable in Flight

Miles high in the air
above brown mountains of Mexico
i take in a wider view
of life and love and letting go

I write these lines
look down again
amazed to see that all has changed
cotton-ball clouds drift
unexpected
Divine Surprise

What's before me on my way?
what blessing
unimagined
is waiting there
just out of sight?

I look again
the clouds are gone
a bony spine snakes down the land

And all alone
as twilight falls
a little town

a cluster of faint lights
nestled in the rugged hills

Who lives down there?
and are they linked
to the bigger, wider world?

Another town now
miles away
no road between
that I can see
from high up here

All we humans are like that
miles apart
looking for the linking roads
so that we can give and take
what we have and what we need:
beauty, warmth, connection, love

Masaje de Curación

Two hours on the table
the body opens to the healing touch
sighs deeply and sinks down

The music shifts
to something soft
and gypsy-like
giving voice to my pain
my heart joins in
with silent tears
mourning the loss
of the dream of us

My soul calls to you
A wordless call
From the soft warm air of Mexico
To the brisk cold wind
Of wherever-you-are

Belly-deep sobs
reach to my core
empty me
bring me peace

I rest
in the calm

Arising from the table now
down the stairs and toward the sea
the sunset lights the sky afire

I see myself reflected there
a living flame of joyous love

This is how I want to be
sharing healing peace and care
private pain transformed to love

Migrations

Our lives first touched in the west
Where molds were shattered
And minds broke free

Now I am a woman of the mountain desert
Earth and fire, high and dry
You are a man of the northern country
Air and water, cold and grey

Far apart we are
in so many ways
how is it that my heart settled on you?
it danced to you on the bridge of music
as we traveled on the path of the heart

My passionate nature is so unlike yours
reserve and abandon, worlds apart
what is the Beloved up to in me
to lead me to such impossibility?
whatever it is, I surrender
Allah's way is deep mystery

An ancient story lives in me
of a life we shared in your northern land

a story of love and separation
heartbreak and lonely exile for me

now I sense coyote working
howling at the desert moon
laughing at the trickster magic
upsetting my world so utterly

But I know coyote isn't cruel
compassion lies at the root of his tricks
he stirs up trouble to open the way
to a deeper reality

You and I will never be lovers
nor partners in the dance of life

But i trust this journey
Through time and space
Leads me to Love's Ecstasy

Buried Treasure

The beauty and light
i see in you
made of you the perfect screen
on which to see my hidden treasure
the buried gifts I hadn't owned

Repeating a pattern decades past
it's the musician in my soul
i saw and heard in you and him
and fell in love with my own gold

Now comes this awakening
i alone can bring it forth
the choir is singing songs I wrote
dances forming one by one

And still there's more for me to see
the lighting of the fire of love of you
opened the way to
lighting the Fire of Love within

Ya Muakhkhir

How like me
to say
goal reached!
inner work done!
Process complete!

I wish

Coming home to myself
in my private world
i cry for you

Despite my wishful thinking
that it's all over and done with
if you came to me in love
i would cast to the wind
in a heartbeat
all thoughts of
could we. . .?
should we. . .?
would we. . .?

and run straight
into your arms

What's the remedy for this pain?
Ya Sabur Ya Matin Ya Azim
to pray for us
Highest Good
for you me her

The vigil continues

Ad-Darr

Dreams die hard

Oh, the death of this dream
is breaking my heart
As did the deaths
of all my loved ones

I suppose
the Beloved
is busy making space
in my being
for more love
more compassion
more joy

But from where I sit now
drenched in tears
that happy ending
seems faint and far away

I have heard
that if you
Drop an r
From Darr
You'll find a door

My beloved teacher said
drop the pain

Maybe
when I've cried enough
I can drop the pain and the r
And walk through the open door

Ya Fattah

Ieri Oggi Domani

I was happy before
part of me was asleep
but i was happy

Now wide awake
having lived this dream
in my heart and mind
for months
only to have it smashed into shards
prayer and practices
bring a measure of peace
but
will i ever be happy
again?

Leaving Mexico
a friend wished me
deep joy, deep joy
as though he caught my pain
be a living flame of joyous love
he taught us all

But first the waters must flow
until the well is dry

Then Insh'Allah
the living flame
will burn clear and bright

On Retreat

I
Al Mumit

I thought
this ritual would be
a celebration
of release
completed

My tears tell me
it isn't over
yet

Insh'Allah
it will give the power
to complete the change

I climb up to my secret sacred place
on the hill
the Seat of Mumit
(The oracle
told me its name)

I put on my white robe
color of death in the eastern world
of purity and new life in the west

I begin with Zikr
chanted and breathed
read aloud
all the poems
chronicle of my heart's journey
chant Ya Mumit
One thousand and one times

I kindle a fire
recite a litany of letting go
burn it—
along with remnants and reminders
of all i wish to leave behind

I remove from my fourth finger
right hand
the ring i put on
the day i came home
from the journey
of my undoing
and never took off
until now

no-one ever knew
why i wore it

I ask the oracle
to lead me to the pathway
i will enter onto
as i emerge from this ceremony

Al Wali'
friendship
perfect

As i shed this skin
of wanting
what i'm not meant to have
may i emerge
shining and new
as a sister
and a friend

I open a book of Rumi's poems
don't move!
a sublime generosity
is coming toward you

I remember
what my Murshid said
let things come to you

The moon is my teacher now

I take prasad from the altar
four pieces of chocolate

for my new relationship to you
for a closer walk with the Beloved
for the unknown delight coming toward me
for Limitless Love
from the depths to the stars

I bury the ashes of the old way
under my heart
on the altar

May the way be opened
to the new

Ya Fattah
Ya Wali'

II
Transition

I did it
i killed my hopes and dreams
they are buried with the ashes
under my heart

Now there is only
emptiness
loneliness

Hafiz says
don't surrender your loneliness
so quickly
let it cut more deep

The old traditional name
for Al Mumit
is The Slayer
behold
one dead dream of love

My sweet old rascal lover
of decades ago
taught about life-giving risk
having to let go

of one trapeze bar
before catching another

So here i am
suspended
in transition

Transition
in birthing
is the hardest time
the loss of one rhythm
before another begins

this is like that
i suppose

Moineddin says
trust

Rumi says
a sublime generosity
is coming toward me

I do dare to believe it
Ya Azim!
divine audacity

I am remembering now
the message coming for months
from all sides
something wonderful
awaits you

it seems that the letting-go
i did today
was of the first trapeze bar

I hope the next one shows up soon

III
Hesitation Step

Wondering is powerful.
—Caroline Casey

Having dropped
the cloak of love
that didn't fit
my heart pauses
in its dance
sways to the music
of wild poets and mystics
drunk with God

I recall
how it is with Rumi
one time lost and lonely
without the Beloved
another time lost in ecstatic Love

Contact high

I wonder
which way
to the Truest Love?

IV
Fruits of the Spirit

Silence

Cliffs and creek
sun, wind, clouds, snow
moon and stars

Zikr and wazaif
thousands of them

I walk the land
i sing and dance
Hu sits

Silence—
only donkeys braying the alfalfa prayer
in the morning
when I step outside the door

Weight lifted
past let go
pain washed away
love transformed

New inspiration
in the open air

Ya Wa'li
loving self-discipline
brings inner freedom

Ya Wali'
a friend to self
a friend to all

La ilaha illa'llah
nothing
only God
Shakur Allah

Silence

Fana-fi-Ishk

Through pain
through joy
through passion
through peace
Love is teaching me Love

Enveloped in cloud
breaking into sunlight
two steps forward
one step back
Love is teaching me Love

I surrender to you my Teacher

On Hearing "Sleeping Beauty"

Pyotr Ilyich Tchaikovsky

How he suffered
in life
and love

How blessed are we
with the beauty
that was birthed from his pain
and his great gift
of moving our hearts with
exquisite melody

Sleeping beauty is
an old and archetypal tale

Something in me
knows this story well

But when i awoke
from that dream
the prince was gone

I'm wide awake now
and there's no going back
to sleep

A Wider View

The psychic says
my love for you
is a catalyst

She says
we are forever linked

She says
we do this for each other

I came in
to do this work
she says

Clearing grief
transforming pain
mine and others'

Opening my heart
stretching

So i may go on
guiding
helping
healing

Thank you
Beloved
for breaking the shell
around my heart
that i may fulfill
my purpose

Fana-fi-Lillah

Break me down
break me all the way down
down to the ground

Grind me to dust
grind me to atoms
make me
as light as air

Lift me up
lift me up higher
lighter than air

Make me
like pieces of cloud
to dissolve
in the sunlight
of Your Love

The Waters

My grief
is a white-sand lagoon
an aquamarine pool
emptying out
into the deep-blue ocean
of all human tears

Crying eases me
washes me out to sea
and wide-open
i cry for all the pain
of the human caravan
past
present
future

Sometimes
tears come
unconnected
to any thought
of personal loss
falling like rain on the ocean

Rain
or outgoing tide
i offer these tears
for the transformation
of all suffering

I come to a place of peace

May peace move
over the face
of the waters

A New Rhythm

I move along in a strange rhythmic dance
two steps forward
one step back

Two long gliding steps in harmony
with the unfolding
of my life in community

Then suddenly
stopped short
a meltdown
thrown into
a contraction
a solitary flood of tears

I'm giving birth to myself

I feel more
i feel naked
i feel new

Layers

Love shows itself
in layers
of increasing lightness

From the densest
earth-earthy
body-wanting

To the flowing
waters of tears

To the rising warmth
of a heart set on fire

To the winds of Spirit-Love
flowing and turning
light as air

I rise
conscious mastery

I sink
confused abandon

Like a bright balloon
over the mountains and deserts
of New Mexico

The more faithful
my practice
the more skilled
the ascending and descending

The rising
is beginning to surpass
the falling

Alhamdulillah!

It Becomes True

Rumi was right
Allah accepts
even counterfeit prayers

They weren't exactly
counterfeit
i sincerely wanted
to be your sister
and your friend

It's just that
other longings
old as my years
kept creeping in
to confuse
and discourage me

The longing
to be touched
to be cherished

But i kept on keeping on
rising and falling
with the updrafts and downdrafts
of Love

Now a new fusion
a form of love
containing
all the layers
is growing in my heart

I can only feel
move
breathe
live

And
it is becoming
true

A Gathering of Sufis

Allah lifted me
out of my small world
high in the air

Landed me gently
in a pool
of wise and loving hearts

The now-and-then tears
were of homecoming
remembrance
of all i have gained
and learned
in twenty years and more
of swimming in this pool

Forgotten for a time
in the fire of this initiation

May i keep on
living with this wider view
unconditional
selfless

universal
flowing like a river
through my heart
to all hearts

Hu Knows

This small heart
broken open
by Love
expands and contracts
in a birthing process
of faith and hope
pain and gritty resolve

Who is this i
that is being born?

Hu is the One
that brought
this about?

How can this flawed vessel
bear
the Power
the Fire
the Light
of this Great Love?

Hu knows

The Border Country

Some old i
is dying
crying as she dies
bathing the heart
in sweet ablution

Nothing is as it was
boundaries stretch
edges melt

The mind can't keep track
is happy to give up
let go
say i don't know

These days
my favorite pose
is forehead to the floor

Watercolors undulate
across my inner eye

Sufi music
wild and sweet
full of heartbreak's ecstasy
is what i long to hear

I say goodbye
to all i was
and all i knew
as i enter the border country
on the pathless path

A faithful fool
in love with Love

Prayer

Prayer is my salvation

Prayers of desperation
O please help me remember
that i am in the
best of Hands
all is well
and all will be well

Prayers of gratitude
pour a healing stream of silver balm
into my crescent moon heart

Prayers for the beloved one
for all beings
dissolve my fixation
on my own little story

Progress the crescent moon to full
this heart that's slowly learning
to Love

Water Blessing

Time to turn over
a new leaf
a new stone
wisdom comes

Decrease what is below
benefit what is above
the lake gives itself up
to green the mountain

The burning field
of my heart
receives
this gentle rain of blessing
comforted
restored

Wet ashes
will fertilize
tender green shoots
new Love
new Life

Ya Wahhabo

A Wider World of Love

An image comes
part prayer
part witnessing
transformation
of love into Love

A container
full of feeling
passion
longing
worn away
by tears
by prayer
by soul work

The walls thin
over time
until one day
they dissolve
without a whisper

Atoms of love
continue to congregate
in the space once bound

Now free
they slowly begin to move
each tiny spark
carries blessing
everywhere

A Wish Come True

By the Grace of Allah
peace descends
blooms within the heart
peace that passes all understanding
peace of surrender
peace of the third Zen Patriarch
life is easy
for those who have no preferences

There is joy
to once again be happy
with what is given

Grace ease joy
that is what he wished for me
his wish has come true
thank you, friend
thank You, Beloved

Al Qahhar

A storm is passing over
thunder and lightning
wind and rain

How like a storm
this journey has been
how like the wild power
of the elements
here in my desert home

Thunder
makes the breath catch
the heart pound

Lightning illuminates
For an instant

Whirling wind
blows away
all that is ungrounded
or no longer living

Driving rain
makes the waters rush
washes everything
clean and new

Then clear skies
sunlight
moonlight
starlight

Peace and silence

The Darshan Tree

This apple tree
is old and gnarled

Life has pruned her
time and again
sometimes harshly
by passing storms
sometimes gently
by hands of loving care

Her life story is written
in the shape of her branches

Last spring
she bloomed for her Beloved
she was covered
in showers of white blossoms
as beautiful as any young bride

Last summer
her abundant fruit
was sweet and nourishing
offered with love
to all who passed by

This spring
unseasonable snow
nipped her flowering
in the bud

This summer
her gifts
will be precious and few

Perhaps next year

Magnificat

(After Coleman Barks' Commentary in
The Drowned Book)

You are my Joseph
my Shams

A great love
met and lost
the fecundating mystery
that opened
then crushed my heart

An immaculate conception
that drowns my separate self
and shapes me as the vessel
of a generation of blessed sorrows
and joys

Oh, how I longed
for a more embodied union!

Like Bahauddin
I know that
deep desire for a beloved one
has its Source

In the primal Ishk
the hunger of all that is holy
for all that is holy

A faint intimation
barely perceptible
sings to me
that after the death and resurrection
comes a union of all desire
that lifts it above and beyond
anything
I have experienced
or understood

Ishk

I am reborn

Ruzbihan says
human love and Divine Love
are not opposites
to choose between

They are two forms
of One Love
if one has the Eyes of Light
to see

One doesn't transfer the love
from one beloved to Another

No, the lover herself
must be transformed

Ash-Shaduan
i testify

This love for you
which long inspired

awakened
wracked
taught me

Keeps on loving

But it is different now

I am the lover
transformed

This love
is now
a deep and quiet high-mountain lake
of loving-kindness
soul-brother mine

No trace of sadness
no hint of longing
gone gone gone
like an early-morning mist
burned away
by the sunfire of Love

As for me
i feel clear as the blue sky
wide awake
wide open
to whatever blessings
my Beloved brings to me

Glossary

Many of the Arabic words in this glossary are wazaif (singular wazifa), also known as the beautiful names of God. Most of them appear in the Qur'an as attributes of the Divine. It is said that they are actually a part of the 999 beautiful names, which are part of the 9,999 beautiful names, and on it goes. Wazaif are usually preceded by either Al- (The), or Ya- (O). Some of them have several meanings; the ones given here are those pertinent to the poem in which they appear. When no language is indicated in this list, the term is Arabic.

Ash-Shaduan - I testify

Baqi – a stripping away, the Real that remains

Alhamdulillah – all of being praises Allah by its very nature; Hallelujah!

Azim – flexible strength; divine audacity

Darr – pain and loss

Darshan – blessing conveyed through the glance of a teacher

Fana-fi-Ishk – in Sufi practice there is a process of greater and greater surrender: Fana-fi-Sheikh, effacement in the teacher, Fana-fi-Rassul, effacement in the Prophet, Fana-fi-Lillah, effacement in God. This is an extension of that of my invention: effacement in Love

Fana-fi-Lillah – see entry above

Fattah – may the Way be opened

Haqq – Truth

Hu – sacred syllable for the Presence of Allah; This Is It

Ieri Oggi Domani – Italian: yesterday, today, tomorrow

Insh'Allah – God willing

Joseph – (Old Testament and Qur'an): in Sufi lore, the beautiful being beloved of Zuleikha, who was awakened spiritually by the transformation of her love for him from selfish to unconditional

Magnificat – Latin: magnifies; from the tradition of Mary's response to the annunciation of Jesus' birth by the angel Gabriel: "My soul doth magnify the Lord"

Masaje de Curacion – Spanish: healing massage

Matin – persistence

Moineddin – Hazrat Pir Moineddin Jablonski (1942-2001), head of the Sufi Ruhaniat International order (then the Sufi Islamia Ruhaniat Society) for 30 years and precious teacher to me

Muakhkhir – delayer, postponer; two steps forward, one step back

Mumit – life-taker; the esoteric meaning of this

name is epitomized by the Sufi saying *"die before you die"*; slaying of the sense of separateness

pbuh – Peace be upon him

Prasad – Sanskrit: edible gift offered to the Divine and then eaten by the devotee, thus taking in the blessing

Pyotr Ilyich Tchaikovsky – 19th century Russian composer; wrote the music for the ballet "Sleeping Beauty"

Qahhar – all-prevailing Divine Power

Rumi – Mevlana Jelaluddin Rumi; 13th century Persian Sufi poet

Ruzbihan - Abu Muhammad Sheikh Ruzbihan Baqli (1128–1209), Persian Sufi poet

Sabur – patience

Shems – dervish and realized being, beloved friend of Rumi, who was himself awakened by his entry into Divine Love with Shems

Solve et coagula – Latin: "dissolve and coagulate"; a principle of Alchemy which means that something must be broken down before it can be coalesced into something higher or more developed. Could be used to describe the process of a caterpillar becoming a butterfly in the chrysalis.

Shakur – gratitude

The Drowned Book – work of Bahauddin, father of Rumi, with commentary by contemporary poet and translator Coleman Barks

Third Zen Partriarch – Sengcan, Chinese 6th-7th century Zen Patriarch

Wahhabo – continuous flow of gifts, favors and blessings

Wa'li - loving self-discipline

Wali' – friendship, the Friend

Wazaif – beautiful Names of God (singular wazifa)

Zikr – remembrance; the phrase "la ilaha illa'llah" (there is nothing but the One Reality); the name of that phrase; the practice of chanting it or placing it on the breath

عشق الله معبود الله

About the Author

Azima Lila Forest has walked the Sufi path for 35 years and serves as a Sheikha (teacher) in that tradition. She is also a Unitarian Universalist minister, a Reiki healing practitioner, and a spiritual retreat guide. She graduated from the University of California at Berkeley and received a Master of Divinity degree from the Starr King School for the Ministry in Berkeley. While a student there 45 years ago, she began the study of dreams and has been working with dreams, hers and others', ever since.

A native of San Francisco, Forest has lived for the past 16 years in the mountain desert town of Silver City in southwestern New Mexico. More information about her work can be found at *www.zianet.com/azima.*

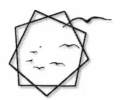

77280319R00077

Made in the USA
Columbia, SC
25 September 2017